Let's
Take a Trip
to the
Very First

Rainbow

ISBN 979-8-88751-285-3 (paperback)
ISBN 979-8-89345-539-7 (hardcover)
ISBN 979-8-88751-286-0 (digital)

Christian Faith Publishing
832 Park Avenue
Meadville, PA 16335
www.christianfaithpublishing.com

Printed in the United States of America

Let's
Take a Trip
to the
Very First

Rainbow

Stacey M. Torres

What is a rainbow? How is it formed? Ever notice you'll see one right after it storms?

Such beautiful colors: red, orange, yellow, blue. But what could they mean though? Maybe rain is a clue!

Let's take a trip back to it's first time revealed. Find out what they're here for the day Earth's fate was sealed.

4

We'll need something small to take us there fast. Let's hop in our airplane and fly back to the past!

There'll be no place to land except on a boat. The one Noah built so the animals could float.

See, God was upset, for the world had turned bad. He decided to flood it and end all that it had.

But a man who's named Noah found favor with God. His choice was to spare him and give him a shot.

God had Noah build a big ark out of wood to house all the creatures he felt that were good.

"Take your wife and your kids, now, quick, go inside! I'm making it rain until all things have died!"

For forty long days, water poured from the skies until all living beings had met their demise.

Many months later, Noah sent out a dove to see if the waters had dried up from the flood.

The bird then returned to the ark with a leaf. "The land must be dry now!" he said with relief.

17

The doors were then opened, and all creatures departed. "Now be fruitful and multiply like when the world first started!"

From that moment on, the Lord made us a promise: He'd never again use the rain to demolish.

He then marked the sky with a beautiful glow. A strip of bright colors He called a rainbow.

"This sign is for all of mankind to recall and always remember my love for you all."

It's time to head home now. It's getting quite late. You now know where rainbows come from, and that's great!

The airplane can land in the yard, and we'll head straight up the stairs, say our prayers, and hop in bed.

Turn off the light, close our eyes, and drift to sleep. And remember, that rainbows are God's promise He'll keep.

Remembering Jenn

81-22

About the Author

Stacey M. Torres was born and raised in Baltimore, Maryland. After closing the military, college, and Texas chapters of her life, she made the bold move to the Midwest this past year to be closer to other family members. She has two children: a four-year-old and an eight-year-old, and just celebrated her tenth wedding anniversary. Her hobbies include minding the homestead she is creating on her new property, reading, and crafting. Stacey is a confirmed member of the Lutheran Church Missouri Synod (LCMS).

9 798887 512853